R ... for Pennies!

Investing in Tax Liens
for Profit and Property

by
Ed C. Tomlinson

Edited by Aimee Fitzgerald
Fagan Business Communications

Cover by Jennifer Willoughby
The National Writers Club

Diamond Publications

5440 Ward Road, Suite 110
Arvada, Colorado 80002

ATTENTION TREASURERS, CORPORATIONS, PROFESSIONAL ORGANIZATIONS, REALTORS, AND UNIVERSITIES: Quantity discounts are available for bulk purchases of this book for educational purposes or fundraising. Special books and book excerpts can also be created to fit specific needs.

For information, please write:

Diamond Publications
5440 Ward Road, Suite 110
Arvada, Colorado 80002

ISBN 0-9626776-4-7
10 9 8 7 6 5 4 3
1st Printing September, 1993

By the same author...

OVERTAXED! Your Guide to Honest Property Tax Reductions by Understanding and Effectively Protesting Your Assessment

DEDICATION

To my wife, Joan, who allowed me to spend time, effort, and financial resources on this project, supporting and believing in me every step of the way.

To the Tomlinson Family:

TODAY
YESTERDAY
TOMORROW

ACKNOWLEDGMENTS

Many people and organizations contributed their thoughts, time, and talents to this book. I am especially grateful to my real estate clients who have sought help from me over the years. Their response to my real estate work has let me know that one person can make a big difference in the world.

My thanks go to the late Don Couch, former treasurer of Jefferson County, and to Jeanne Thorne, who helped motivate me to begin this project. I am also grateful to Gordon Pierce for his invaluable guidance.

My appreciation is also extended to the key individuals who assisted me with the production of this book: Aimee Fitzgerald, Drew Myron, and my wife, Joan, for their help with writing and editing; Pat Hake, for layout; and Dave Black, who made sure the printing was perfect.

I owe special thanks to all those who helped me write my first critically acclaimed, best-selling book, *OVERTAXED! Your Guide to Honest Property Tax Reductions by Understanding and Effectively Protesting Your Assessment,* and in particular to my editor, Aimee Fitzgerald.

TABLE OF CONTENTS

INTRODUCTION

Obtaining real estate for the price of its property taxes?! There must be a catch, you say. Something more to it? One of those get-rich-quick schemes from a late-night real estate show, perhaps?

The answer to each of those questions is an emphatic "NO!" In fact, not only is it possible to obtain real estate for the price of the property taxes owed on it, it's legal, simple, and straight-forward! And in doing so, you will not only be making a personal investment, but also doing a public service!

Buying real estate for only the price of its property taxes actually involves buying the lien on a property carrying unpaid taxes. By paying the amount of the unpaid tax bill to the treasurer of the county in which the property resides, the purchaser becomes the owner of the assignment of the county's lien against the property.

At some future point in time, the property owner will most likely pay those taxes back to the county - along with interest, which happens to accrue at a **substantially** higher rate than conventional investment products. Upon receipt of the payment, the county treasurer contacts the lienholder to redeem the lien. Acting only as a "middleman," the treasurer then gives the lienholder a check for the full amount of the back taxes and interest as received from the delinquent property owner!

If the property owner does not pay those back taxes within the next three years, the lienholder can file for a deed to the property. It's that simple: an easy investment with minimal risk for up to three years, followed by a chance to own real property for a price usually representing only a fraction of its real value.

As many as 15,000 property tax liens are sold to the public each year in Colorado, covering millions of dollars of unpaid taxes. You may find some of my own experiences convincing - and you may be as surprised as I was to learn why and how this situation occurs.

Many years ago, eager to broaden my real estate knowledge and track down new sales leads, I acquired a tax lien list. I naively assumed that these property owners couldn't afford to pay their taxes, but quickly learned that this was not true in most cases. Some weren't paying because they didn't even know they owned the property! But many - if not most - others were actually utilizing the tax lien sale procedure as an alternative to obtaining a conventional bank loan!

To further broaden my real estate knowledge and satisfy my curiosity, I attended a tax lien sale in Jefferson County. It took only 30 minutes to realize how easy the process is. As I had some cash with me, I deposited it with the county treasurer's office, and, as a learning experience, purchased three tax liens at that sale. When they were later redeemed, I did indeed receive all my money back, as promised - with substantial interest!

A year later, I contacted my banker and told him of my discovery. He gave me an unsecured personal loan, with payback to come from the redemptions of the liens. In fact, he was so impressed with the idea that **he** started doing it! Today, he owns a number of mountain cabins through his lien investing! A client to whom I introduced the idea bought 12 tax liens and ended up owning a small strip of land under a large florist shop.

In attending another tax lien sale in Jefferson County, I purchased 40 tax liens on small vacant land properties with my loan. I realized that chances of redemption would increase greatly if buildings were erected on the land. The result? Forty percent of the properties were redeemed within the first year!

Along with 37 redemptions from those liens, I acquired 3 property deeds. One is an unbuildable lot near the heart of Evergreen - that's all I know about its location. But I do know that it is only a matter of time before someone combines several of these lots to make one large enough on which to build. My plan is to simply hold the property as an asset until that time.

The other two deeds were for a parcel of land and an interest in mineral rights. While I still don't know where they are located, what's important is that eventually, I know that someone will contact me, as the owner, to see if I wish to sell.

In fact, a wonderful elderly man did contact me recently regarding the mineral rights deed, which turned out to be located in Golden Gate Canyon. I turned down his reasonable purchase offer at the time, even though I would have made a 1,500 percent profit! In retrospect, I probably should have taken it.

On the third deed, a Colorado Springs Realtor contacted me to inform me of an entity that might have a sincere interest in purchasing it - the Denver Water Department! I then learned my property was 376 feet below the proposed Two Forks reservoir! I sold it for over a 2,250 percent profit.

Another great experience occurred many months after gambling was approved in Central City. I stopped by the treasurer's office with my client and good friend, Hal McNutt of Arvada, to see what we could discover on property tax sales. What a surprise! We found nearly 100 tax liens that were never sold at prior sales! We quickly and easily identified which ones were in the cities of Black Hawk and Central City - and never took the time to find out the exact property locations. Did I end up purchasing the liens? Learning the exact property locations? Owning the properties? If you ever run into me, ask me and I'll tell you!

These are only a few of my experiences with the property tax lien system. They are not unique, nor limited to real estate professionals. This book is designed for **you** - young, old, rich, or poor. It is for anyone who wants to understand and learn how to invest in property tax liens. Read on!

Chapter 1

HOW THE TAX LIEN SYSTEM WORKS: AN OVERVIEW

Treasurers are essentially bill collectors who serve as county bankers. They have nothing to do with determining the amount of property taxes due. The county assessor delivers a tax list and warrant to the county treasurer, noting the collection data. The treasurer simply collects the taxes due, invests the funds received, and disburses the funds to the taxing districts.

What Happens with Unpaid Property Taxes

In Colorado, property taxes for the prior year are due in a lump sum payment by April 30. If a property owner wishes to pay in installments, the first half is due February 28 and the second half June 15. No installments are accepted for tax bills under $25.

No later than September 1, the treasurer notifies delinquent taxpayers of unpaid taxes. Property owners must respond within 10 days. Twenty days after mailing the notices, the treasurer makes a list of taxpayers (and properties) who have not responded. Those are the tax liens which will be offered for sale to the public. In Colorado, tax lien sales occur each year in October, November, or early December. Each county sets its own sale date. Treasurers offer these tax liens for sale in hopes that investors will buy them and thereby pay the taxes due.

Buying a Tax Lien as an Investment

The typical tax sale is held as an auction, as there will generally be more than one person wishing to purchase a particular lien. The winning bidder receives a recorded Certificate of Purchase. Interest on that Certificate starts accruing from the day of the auction, and is paid on a monthly basis. The interest accrues until the property owner pays the back taxes (and accrued interest) to the treasurer.

At that time, the treasurer sends a note to the Certificate of Purchase holder requesting surrender of the Certificate. On receipt of the Certificate, the treasurer sends the lienholdler a check for the full amount paid, plus interest, as received from the delinquent taxpayer.

Interest Rates

The tax lien sale system works for one reason: It makes sense for investors to buy the liens. With interest rates on tax liens typically running eight percentage points above those for a one-year certificate of deposit (see Appendix A), it makes sense to buy them.

The annual rate of interest on tax liens is set at nine percentage points above the discount rate, the rate of interest a commercial bank pays to the Federal Reserve Bank. Interest paid is simple interest, and is not compounded annually.

The state commissioner of banking establishes the annual rate of interest based on the computation specified above. The rate is established each September 1, and becomes effective October 1. The same interest rates apply statewide.

Interest on Certificates of Purchase starts accruing the moment the tax lien is sold. As mentioned, even if an owner is at the treasurer's office paying his/her tax bill as the lien is being sold, the lienholder will still receive a full month's interest. This is because interest always accrues from the first of the month for the entire month. No matter when during the month the owner pays the back taxes, the entire month's interest is due. That full amount, in turn, will go to the lienholder when the Certificate is redeemed.

Interest is assessed against the total tax amount due. Interest continues to accrue for 15 years if the property owner does not pay the outstanding balance. If the lienholder does not apply for a deed to the property (see below) within 15 years, the lien will be cancelled by the treasurer using a Certificate of Cancellation, and the lienholder loses the entire investment.

Acquiring the Property

Certificate holders do not hold rights to properties. They are simply lienholders who hope to be paid back. But if the property owner continues to neglect his/her yearly taxes, the certificate holder may continue to pay the taxes on his/her behalf. After paying for three years, the certificate holder may apply for a treasurer's deed to the property - thereby becoming the owner of the property.

Actually, the original certificate holder may not even have to pay subsequent taxes to apply for a deed! If s/he purchased the original lien, but did not choose to pay the back taxes in subsequent years, the lien would, of course, be resold to another bidder at a tax lien sale. That new lienholder would become a "junior" lienholder. When the time comes to apply for a deed, the original, or "senior," lienholder, maintains a priority to apply over the junior lienholder. The senior lienholder would simply have to reimburse the junior lienholder(s) for the amount of the taxes paid (plus interest).

Before issuing a deed to a property, the treasurer's office will attempt to locate and notify the owner through a variety of methods. The treasurer will also confirm that the person noted is the owner of record. If, after several months, the owner or those who have an interest in the property have not paid the full tax amount due (with interest), the treasurer will issue a Treasurer's Deed, granting the certificate holder full rights to the property.

Chapter 2

BUT IS IT FAIR?

Potential investors in tax liens might wonder if the system offers a fair method of earning money and obtaining property. The answer: Yes!

Selling property for the price of its taxes can be a win-win situation for all parties involved. First and foremost, it is the mechanism that ensures that all taxing districts receive the tax revenue due them. Without property tax income, these districts can not provide normal and customary services to residents. And without the tax lien method of obtaining the tax money, all of us who pay taxes on time would have to make up the difference. And we are talking about large amounts of money here. In Colorado's larger counties, property tax liens total over several million dollars of uncollected taxes annually!

For the lien purchaser, the system makes excellent business sense because of the high interest rates involved. Investors are, in effect, lending the property owner money to pay his/her back taxes. The delinquent taxpayer's obligation and burden is not only the total tax bill, but the high interest which accrues on the unpaid taxes. As explained, that interest - from which the investor will ultimately benefit - bears a much higher rate than money borrowed from a bank.

So, you say, maybe lien purchases make sense. But what about acquiring actual property for only the price of those unpaid taxes? You will recall that if the delinquent property owner does not pay back taxes for the next three years, the lienholder is eligible to apply for a deed to the property. While the process is relatively simple, it doesn't happen quickly. Numerous safeguards must be exercised to protect owners from losing their properties in this manner. Yet, hundreds of property owners do lose their properties for one of several reasons:

- The owner(s) did not know s/he owned the property. For instance, a woman in Boulder thought she had sold all of the land she owned near the Coors brewery in Golden. The legal description in the deed, however, excluded about one-half acre. In nearby Arvada, a widow thought her late husband had sold an empty lot next to an apartment building along with the building. As it turned out, she still owned the lot.

- The taxes payable each year exceed the value of the property. In these cases, assessors have mistakenly overvalued the property for tax purposes.

- The owner(s) simply does not have the money to pay the property taxes. Even here, safeguards exist to protect against loss of a home, including tax deferral and work-off programs for those 65 years of age and older.

- When a property has been damaged beyond repair, an uninsured owner sometimes just gives up.

- If so many liens accumulate on the property that the owner cannot sell it and pay everyone off, s/he may give up. If no one lienholder chooses to own the property through foreclosure, the lienholder can apply for the deed.

- The land is contaminated and requires extensive clean-up too expensive to warrant paying the taxes. Examples include property containing tailings from abandoned mines, and industrial areas in which solvents or other chemicals have been found.

- The owner(s) has died, leaving no heirs.

- The owner(s) has moved without leaving a forwarding address.

Chapter 3

WHO BUYS TAX LIENS?

Almost anyone can purchase property tax liens. Classrooms of elementary school children have been known to attend tax sales. Sometimes corporations are formed to pool money. Other participants include investment pools, churches, investment clubs, individuals investing for Individual Retirement Accounts, and, on occasion, professional investors. It is not uncommon to see representatives from banks at sales, bidding on behalf of a corporation for the bank. They, too, understand a good investment when they see one. Bidders need not be residents of the county in which they purchase liens.

Elected and appointed county officials, county employees, and members of their immediate families may not participate in the tax lien sale process (see Section 18-1-106, Colorado Revised Statutes, 1973). One exception to this policy occurs if a property was owned by the county official, employee, or family member before the sale of a tax lien, or if the property is located within a county other than the county in which the official is elected, appointed or employed.

Knowingly violating tax sale acquisition regulations is a misdemeanor punishable by Section 18-1-106, Colorado Revised Statues, 1973.

Chapter 4

PURCHASING TAX LIENS: HOW TO GET STARTED

Contact your county treasurer's office (see Appendix B) to learn the date of the next tax lien sale. Sales in each of Colorado's 63 counties are usually held between October 1 and December 15 of each year.

Ask the treasurer which newspaper will carry the list of property tax liens to be sold at that sale. You can also obtain the list directly from the treasurer's office. Each county's specific bidding rules are included in this publication.

If you want to know the probable rules for a specific county before publication of the lists, simply contact the treasurer's office of the desired county and inquire which newspaper published last year's list. Then contact the newspaper to purchase the back issue. The rules are not likely to change much from one year to the next.

Chapter 5

REVIEWING TAX LIEN SALE LISTINGS

The tax lien sale lists you obtain will usually contain the following information for each property:

- an identification number, usually called a schedule number
- name of the current owner
- legal description, which may include:
  - » subdivision name
  - » lot number and block number within the subdivision
  - » location coordinates, called Section, Township, Range, Quarter, and, sometimes, Key
- amount of acreage (in some cases)
- a notation as to whether the tax sale lien has been previously offered (in some cases)
- a notation as to whether the property is vacant land, "improved" (buildings exist on it), or consist of mineral rights

- value - the assessor's assessed valuation, not the "actual value" (see Glossary)
- amount of property taxes due
- fees, interest, and other costs due
- total amount due (taxes, fees, interest, and other costs)

Property Addresses

Note that the exact address of the property may not be noted on the list. Actually, many tax liens in Colorado are for vacant land, which does not even have an address assigned to it. Because as many as 50 percent of your liens may be redeemed within six months, the time and effort it takes to research the exact location of the property is generally not worth the effort.

If, however, you find yourself holding liens at the end of a year, you should research those locations to be sure you have an interest in eventually owning the property before you invest additional money. Also, make sure you know what you are bidding on if you are aggressively seeking expensive liens.

Section, Township, and Range Numbers

To learn the location of a property, you will need to learn how to use section, township, and range numbers.

To start, obtain a county map with an overlap of section, township, and range numbers (see Appendix C). These maps are available at the county mapping department, assessor's office, or any number of outdoor/sporting goods retail outlets.

Range numbers run across the top of the map while township numbers run along the side. Six miles exist between each range number and between each township number. The 36 smaller numbers in the square boxes are section numbers, each representing one square mile.

The legal description may also contain designations for northwest (NW), southwest (SW), northeast (NE), and southeast (SE). These designations represent the quarter section in which the property is located.

Check with the county assessor's office (or a high school geography teacher) to learn how to specifically locate a property on your maps if you cannot figure it out. While it may appear confusing at first, you will find it simple once you understand the system.

Note that while the section/township/range system is utilized worldwide, some counties have their own mapping systems. If you encounter this, ask the assessor's or treasurer's office for assistance.

Chapter 6

THE SALE

One-Two Days Prior to the Sale

If you intend to purchase a tax lien at a public sale, you must deposit money and obtain both a receipt and tax sale auction number at the county treasurer's office on or before the day of the sale. While some treasurers' offices will open early on the sale date to accommodate depositers, I recommend you deposit your funds a day or two prior so that you are more relaxed and have good seating on the day of the sale.

The form of payment accepted is determined by each county treasurer's rules, but usually includes cash, certified checks, money orders, cashier's checks, or personal checks (if guaranteed by a bank's irrevocable letter of credit placed on file ahead of time at the treasurer's office).

Remember the original tax lien sale list you obtained? The county will update the list daily until the sale date and post the updates at the county treasurer's office. Property owners who have paid back taxes since the original publication will be stricken from the list. This number might total about 15 percent of the liens up for sale. If you are determined to obtain a specific lien, you will need to check the updates just prior to the sale to see if it is still available.

Arriving at the Sale

Seating at the sale is determined by the treasurer's rules, and may be open, assigned or reserved. Arrive a little early to get a good seat. When attending your first tax lien sale, just watch for 15 minutes or so. You will be surprised to find how quickly you will get a feel for how it works and how much your self-confidence will increase.

The Bidding Procedure

During the auction, the treasurer's staff will keep track of your winning bids to determine if you have sufficient funds on deposit. Once your deposit balance is used, you are no longer recognized as a bidder unless you choose to deposit funds on the spot (assuming such action does not delay the tax lien sale and is acceptable to the treasurer).

Treasurers have broad powers to set bidding rules. Most counties simply handle the bidding as an auction, but for liens under $5,000, bidders may be assigned numbers to implement a rotating bid system. If your turn comes and the lien for sale is not of interest to you, the bidding will continue to move to the next person in rotation until a bid is made.

The sequence of bidding usually follows the most up-to-date published tax lien list. Keep in mind that when a person makes a bid, it simply means that s/he is bidding for the right to pay the tax. Bidding is usually referenced by the property schedule or identification number.

All bids automatically assume that you are agreeing to pay the total amount due. For some large properties, such as shopping centers, the tax amount due could easily be more than $50,000. In contrast, the total amount due on tiny pieces of land may total only a few dollars. If you are the only bidder for a given lien, simply state, "Flat," which means you wish to pay the amount due with no premiums (see below).

Bidding continues until all the liens have been sold, until no investor interest remains in liens offered, or until the close of business. If tax liens remain on the docket at the end of the day, bidding resumes the following business day. All bids are final, with no changes or cancellations.

Premiums

Some treasurers may require a minimum bid (usually $1), known as a "premium." This is above the total amount due. During the bidding, you will usually hear bids of $1 over the amount due, and higher if there is more than one bidder. Premiums are not refundable at any time, nor is any interest paid on premiums. This is simply risk money.

Bidding with premiums usually takes place in increments of dollars. If the tax bill is very large, the auctioneer may request bidders make premium offers in increments of $25. Premiums can amount to a figure totaling several percent of the total amount due. They go directly to the county's general fund to be "wisely spent" by the board of county commissioners (a little humor from the late Don Couch, former treasurer of Jefferson County.)

As a rule of thumb, premiums become smaller toward the end of the sale, as many bidders use up their money and/or leave the sale. Those who do stay may have less money left with which to bid.

You will find that some investors make no premium bids, or bids only up to the amount of one month's interest on the lien. This ensures a modest gain in the event a purchased lien is redeemed quickly. Remember that even if redemption occurs one day after the sale, the lienholder will still receive a full month's interest.

Unsold Liens

Most tax liens are sold, but in the event a lien remains unsold after a sale, the county will usually strike (not collect/not pay the taxing district due) the taxes due and hold the lien itself. If the county holds the lien for 30 years, in which time no investor has come forward to purchase the lien, it will return the lien to sale via a Certificate of Cancellation. The county also has the non-exclusive option to buy the lien after the sale in hopes of eventually acquiring the property (for their own use or to resell and collect the taxes due).

Note that not all existing property tax liens will be put up for sale. For example, a treasurer may decide that a piece of land is worthless. Liens on properties in bankruptcy and on properties held by the Resolution Trust Corporation may not be offered for sale to the public because the treasurer is requesting payment of unpaid taxes directly from the bankruptcy court or the Resolution Trust Corporation.

While it usually requires the permission of the county commissioners, the treasurer often maintains the authority to conduct the sale of unsold liens (assignments) via a standing order of acceptance. If the amount due exceeds $10,000, the sale must be advertised and approved by the State Division of Property Taxation.

Chapter 7

AFTER THE SALE

Obtaining Refunds on Deposits

Within a few days, the treasurer will refund any deposited money not used at the sale. To insure a prompt refund, be sure to fill out the initial information carefully when you go to deposit your money. Refunds are usually very prompt so that investors can more easily attend other counties' sales. In fact, treasurers and their staffs have even been known to work on weekends to process the refund paperwork!

Obtaining a Receipt and Certificate of Purchase

Within a few days, the treasurer may send receipts for the winning bids to the appropriate investors. If, by chance, the lien an investor buys is paid during those days, the investor will still receive a check with one month's interest.

Investors with winning bids will receive a Certificate of Purchase about two weeks after the sale, allowing time to properly record the lien in county records. The Certificate of Purchase certifies an individual as the lienholder. It is also the document that must be surrendered to redeem the lien if and when the property owner pays the back taxes. The Certificate is valuable and transferable, meaning it can be sold or assigned to another person. It can also be placed in a will. A lienholder can even borrow against it.

The Following Years

Each July, the treasurer's office will notify lienholders by mail if the taxes on the Certificate are again unpaid. The lienholder can then pay the amount due without any bidding. If a lienholder chooses not to pay the amount due, a new "junior" lien on the property will be offered to another bidder at the next sale.

Chapter 8

REDEMPTION OF LIENS

Procedure

All transactions regarding the property owner and the funds collected at the tax sale are handled through the treasurer's office. The property owner pays his/her taxes to the treasurer, not to the lienholder directly. Often, the property owner never even sees the lienholder's name, although it is a matter of public record.

When a property owner pays his/her back taxes, the treasurer will notify the lienholder by mail. The lien-holder can return the Certificate of Purchase by mail or in person. A lienholder who goes to the treasurer's office in person can usually receive a check in just a few minutes. A Certificate of Redemption is issued to the property owner (or mortgage company) who paid the redemption.

A drawback to the system is that the investor's money is tied up for an indefinite amount of time, as one never knows if or when the property owner will pay the back taxes. The investor, a lender of sorts, has no control over when the money is paid back. As redemption occurs whenever the property owner pays his/her back taxes to the county, the investor can go unpaid for years.

Redeeming an Erroneously Sold Lien

Although the county rarely makes a mistake, it does occur sometimes. One example would be a tax lien offered for sale on a property which actually has no taxes due. If, at any time, the county finds it erroneously sold a tax lien, it will reimburse the investor the total funds paid plus modest interest (two percent above the discount rate). Premiums are not refunded.

Chapter 9

OBTAINING THE DEED TO A PROPERTY

Filing for the Deed

If a property owner does not pay his/her taxes for three years from the date on which the lien was first offered, the original (senior) lienholder - or any junior lienholders - may apply for issuance of a "Notice of Purchase of Real Estate at Tax Sale and of Application for Issuance of Treasurer's Deed" to take possession of the property. (The process can be started before the three years have expired, but the deed cannot be finalized until the period has elapsed.) If a junior lienholder files for the deed, s/he must pay off the senior lienholder. If the senior lienholder applies for the deed, s/he must redeem the junior lienholder's position.

The fee with this application is determined by each county treasurer, but is usually a few hundred dollars. The exact amount is dependent on the cost of the title search, amount of certified mail required, and the cost of advertising. Once the treasurer receives the completed application and fee, s/he will order a title search on the property to ensure that the name listed is the owner of record and to identify any other parties with an interest in the property. S/he will also run three consecutive weekly advertisements in a local newspaper to notify the public that the property is under consideration for deed transfer. Applicants are encouraged to check out the property's condition and fair market value before applying for a deed to help ensure a good investment.

State law requires that the treasurer's office also notify any occupants of the premises, as well as the person to whom the property is assessed and all persons having an interest or lien of record on the property. The law requires the treasurer to utilize reasonable diligence in the notification process. Anyone with a legal interest in the property is eligible to pay the amounts due to protect their interest in the property.

Three-five months after the first notification to the property owner (through newspaper advertising or certified mail), if no payments are made, the county treasurer will notify the lienholder of issuance of the deed. Should the property owner, or someone with a legal interest, pay the amounts due during this time, all filing fees will be refunded to the lienholder.

Some lienholders pay the taxes for years and never apply for the deed. If you want to apply for a deed on one of these properties, the treasurer's office may copy its list of lienholders for you or conduct research to identify these lienholders (for a fee). Once you have identified a lienholder on a property you desire, you can then negotiate for an assignment of the lien with that lienholder.

Once a deed is issued, all liens and previous encumbrances (mortgages) are extinguished. Any claims to the property via adverse possession or squatters rights are also extinguished. Also, once the deed is issued, the new owner may find it worthwhile to determine the exact location and boundaries of the property with the assistance of a professional surveyor.

Integrity of the Deed

A treasurer's deed to a property issued through payment of taxes due is good, but not perfect. It is possible that a prior owner could surface and try to lay claim to the property (through a court of law). S/he would have to prove that s/he was under legal disability at the time of deed transfer. The previous owner has five-nine years from the date of deed transfer to accomplish this. Should a prior owner prove his/her case, the deedholder would be reimbursed all acquisition expenses plus 15 percent interest. In addition, the prior owner must reimburse the deedholder for any improvements made to the property (at the present value of such improvements).

It is also possible, but not probable, that a prior owner could show due cause to overturn the deed if the treasurer did not comply with the laws of the state in offering the lien for sale, or did not process and execute a proper search for prior owners or other legally interested parties before completing the transaction. Such events are rare.

Taking Possession

With deed in hand, the lienholder has full control over the property in its **current** condition at time of acquisition. If, by chance, someone is using the property or living on it, the property owner may need to call the police for trespassing and/or start eviction proceedings. Most evictions take three weeks.

As a new property owner, you can now sell the property if you wish to do so. By offering a "quit claim deed" on the property to a potential buyer, you will not need title insurance to complete the transaction. A quit claim deed simply conveys any and all interest you have in the property to the buyer, but does not provide any guarantees of ownership. If your buyer wants a guarantee of ownership, you may offer a "general warranty deed," which is a guarantee that the deed is good and can not be challenged successfully.

Title Insurance

Title insurance protects you from your deed being faulty. Most title companies will not offer title insurance to a property owner until s/he has held the deed five-nine years (from the date of issuance of the treasurer's deed). To speed that process, contact an attorney to do a "quiet title suit," a process that clears the deed of any possible defects. Most title companies will offer insurance once this is completed.

Property Tax Assessment

Once the deed is in hand, check the assessor's valuation for accuracy in his/her property tax assessment (see *OVERTAXED!*). If you find it's way off, protest the assessment with the county assessor's office.

Volume of Deed Transactions

To get an idea of just how many properties are held by owners with treasurer's deeds, I did some research into county records. About one percent of all liens sold end up with a deed. With 1,000 - 2,000 liens sold each year in large counties (many more in bad economic years), I estimate that 100 - 200 deeds are awarded each year statewide. Many of these properties have been resold and are no longer easily identified, but the facts on those that **can** be identified are impressive.

In Jefferson County, 265 recorded treasurer's deeds existed as of April, 1993. Of those, 260 are for vacant land. Statistics are impressive: 50 deeds are for properties ranging from a lot size up to an acre; 26 are for properties of 1 - 5 acres; 17 are 6 - 45 acres; and 2 are over 120 acres in size! The five improved properties have minor structures built on them.

Although Denver County's data base is incomplete, 25 of 29 I located have improvements. Almost half of those are dwelling units.

In Arapahoe County, 166 treasurer's deeds are currently recorded, including some with up to several acres of land.

In Boulder County, 123 Treasurer's deeds are currently recorded. Of those, four are dwelling units. Of the 119 vacant land properties, many are at least a lot size, and some exceed 40 acres.

AFTERWORD

By now, you should have a fairly good grasp of the tax lien system and good understanding of how you can obtain a very handsome interest rate, and on occasion, real estate for the price of property taxes. You should also understand that the system usually provides a win-win situation for all parties involved, and that it actually provides a means of public service by helping to maintain an orderly flow of ownership and taxation - all accomplished with safeguards for the property owner.

You may find, as I have, that some serious tax lien investors are reluctant to talk about their recent experiences. This situation appears to stem from recent changes in the tax lien system. As the sale system becomes more well-known, it attracts more investors. Sales, therefore, attract more bidders, and more bidders lead to higher premiums. Some long-time investors may yearn for the "good old days" when sales were poorly attended and premiums were lower (or non-existent). To insure as many members of the public can participate in the system on an equitable basis, it is my hope that we will see a greater use of rotational bidding throughout our counties.

Also, remember that attendance at sales varies from year to year, depending on interest rates and publicity.

Don't give up: The tax lien system provides a reasonably sound investment and should be repeated annually.

A word of caution: Know what you are buying. Be careful not to acquire a tax lien or a deed if it costs more than the property is worth! *Caveat emptor.*

My best to you in all your real estate ventures. May all of your investments in property tax liens be as good as mine.

Appendix A

INTEREST RATES

	Tax Lien	One-Year Certificate of Deposit* (as of October 1)
1980	23%	
1981	19 %	
1982	18 %	
1983	18%	
1984	17%	
1985	15 %	
1986	15 %	
1987	15%	7.001%
1988	16%	7.500%
1989	16%	8.000%
1990	16%	7.125%
1991	15%	5.625%
1992	12%	3.375%
1993 (est.)	12%	3.250%

*Source: First Bank of West Arvada

Appendix B

COLORADO COUNTY TREASURERS' OFFICES

Adams
  450 S. 4th Ave., Brighton, C0 80601
  303-659-2120

Alamosa
  402 Edison Ave., Alamosa, C0 81101
  719-589-3626

Arapahoe
  5334 S. Prince, Littleton, C0 80166
  303-795-4550

Archuleta
  449 San Juan St., Pagosa Springs, C0 81147
  303-264-2152

Baca
  741 Main St., Springfield, C0 81073
  719-523-4262

Bent
    725 Bent Ave., Las Aminas, C0 81054
    719-456-2211

Boulder
    1350 Spruce, Boulder, C0 80306
    303-441-3520

Chaffee
    104 Crestone Ave., Salida, C0 81201
    719-539-6808

Cheyenne
    51 S.1st St., Cheyenne Wells, C0 80810
    719-767-5657

Clear Creek
    405 Argentine, Georgetown, C0 80444
    303-569-3251

Conejos
    6683 County Rd. 13, Conejos, C0 81129
    719-376-5919

Costilla
    352 Main St., San Luis, C0 81152
    719-672-3342

Crowley
    6th & Main, Ordway, C0 81063
    719-267-4624

Custer
    205 S. 6th, Westcliffe, C0 81252
    719-783-2341

Delta
    5th & Palmer, Delta, Co 81416
    303-874-4449

Denver
   144 W. Colfax, # 310, Denver, C0 80202
   303-640-2555

Dolores
   409 Main, Dove Creek, C0 81324
   303-677-2386

Douglas
   301 Wilcox St., Castle Rock, C0 80104
   303-660-7455

Eagle
   500 Broadway, Eagle, C0 81631
   303-328-8868

Elbert
   215 Comanche St., Kiowa, C0 80117
   303-621-2104

El Paso
   27 E. Vermigo, Colo. Springs, C0 80901
   719-520-6691

Fremont
   615 Macon, Canon City, C0 81212
   719-275-1521

Garfield
   109 8th St., Glenwood Springs, CO 81602
   303-945-6382

Gilpin
   203 Eureka St., Central City, C0 80427
   303-582-5222

Grand
   308 Byers, Hot Sulphur Springs, C0 80451
   303-725-3347

Gunnison
> 200 E. Virginia, Gunnison, C0 81230
> 303-641-2231

Hinsdale
> 308 Hinson St., Lake City, CO 81235
> 303-944-2223

Huerfano
> 401 Main, Walsenberg, CO 81089
> 719-738-1280

Jackson
> 396 LaFever, Walden, CO 80480
> 303-723-4220

Jefferson
> 100 Jefferson County Parkway, Golden, CO 80419
> 303-271-8330

Kiowa
> 1200 Goff, Eads, CO 81036
> 719-438-5831

Kit Carson
> 251 16th St., Burlington, CO 80807
> 719-346-8434

Lake
> 505 Harrision Ave., Leadville, CO
> 719-486-0530

La Plata
> 1060 2nd Ave., Durango, CO 81302
> 303-259-4000

Larimer
> 200 W. Oak, Fort Collins, CO 80522
> 303-498-7020

Las Aminas
    1st & Maple St., Trinidad, CO 81082
    719-846-2981

Lincoln
    103 3rd Ave., Hugo, CO 80821
    719-743-2633

Logan
    300 Ash, Sterling, CO 80751
    303-522-2462

Mesa
    544 Road Ave. Grand Junction, CO 81501
    303-244-1833

Mineral
    2nd & Main St., Creed, CO 81130
    719-658-2325

Moffat
    221 W. Victory Way, Craig, CO 81626
    303-824-6670

Montezuma
    109 W. Main, Cortez, CO 81321
    303-565-7550

Montrose
    320 S. First St., Montrose, CO 81402
    303-249-3565

Morgan
    231 Ensign St., Fort Morgan, CO 80701
    303-867-8524

Otero
    Third & Colorado Ave., La Junta, CO 81050
    719-384-5473

Ouray
   541 4th St., Ouray, CO 81427
   303-325-4487

Park
   501 Main, Fairplay, CO 80440
   719-836-2771

Phillips
   221 S. Interocean Ave., Holyoke, CO 80734
   303-854-2822

Pitkin
   506 E. Main, Aspen, CO 81611
   303-920-5200

Prowers
   301 S. Main, Lamar, CO 81052
   719-336-2081

Pueblo
   210 W. 10th, Pueblo, CO 81003
   719-546-6000

Rio Blanco
   555 Main St., Meeker, CO 81641
   303-878-3614

Rio Grande
   6th & Cherry, Del Norte, CO 81132
   719-657-2747

Routt
   522 Lincoln Ave., Steamboat Springs, CO 80477
   303-879-1732

Saguache
   501 4th St., Saguache, C0 81149
   719-655-2656

San Juan
>   1557 Greene, Silverton, CO 81433
>   303-387-5488

San Miguel
>   305 W. Colorado Ave., Telluride, CO 81435
>   303-728-4451

Sedgwick
>   3rd & Cedar St., Julesburg, CO 80737
>   303-474-3473

Summit
>   208 Lincoln, Breckenridge, CO 80424
>   303-453-2561

Teller
>   101 W. Bennat, Cripple Creek, CO 80813
>   719-689-2985

Washington
>   150 Ash St., Akron, CO 80720
>   303-345-6601

Weld
>   1400 N.17th Ave., Greeley, CO 80631
>   303-353-3845

Yuma
>   130 Ash St., Wray, CO 80758
>   303-332-4965

Appendix C

Map of Range, Township, and Section

Jefferson County, R70W T02S Section 1-36

R70W (West)

120th Ave

06	05	04	03	02	01
07	08	09	WESTMINSTER 10	11	12
18	17	16	15	14	13
19	20	* 21	22	23	24
30	29	28	27	26	25
31	32	33	34	ARVADA 35	36

↑ N

T02S (South)

88th Ave

72nd Ave

Indiana Kipling Wadsworth Sheridan

* R70W T02S S21 (Standley Lake)

GLOSSARY

A

Actual Value--the dollar value assigned to a property by the county assessor. It is not the property's current fair market value. Also called "assessor's appraisal," "total actual value," "appraisal," "appraised value," and "assessor's value."

Adverse Possession--property rights obtained when a person uses someone else's land, unchallenged, for over 16 years.

Assessment--an official valuation of real property for tax purposes, based on appraisals.

Assessment Rate--the percentage of a property's actual value (assessor's) used to calculate a property's assessed value, or assessment.

Assessed Valuation--a percentage of the assessor's actual value for tax purposes. Multiplying the actual value by the assessment rate determines the assessment.

C

Certificate of Cancellation-- (1) the document which reverses the issuance of a Certificate of Purchase. (2) the document which returns an unsold lien to the county tax sale. (3) the document issued when a junior lienholder obtains a deed from a senior lienholder.

Certificate of Purchase--the document showing proof of ownership of a tax lien.

Certificate of Redemption--the document showing proof of payment on the tax lien.

E

Encumbrances--a generic term for liens against a property.

F

Flat--the verbal expression used to represent the agreement of paying only the amount owed at a treasurer's tax lien sale.

G

General Warranty Deed--a deed that guarantees that the deed is good and can not be challenged successfully.

I

Identification Number--see "Schedule Number"

Investment Clubs--see "Investment Pools"

Investment Pools--groups of people who invest money jointly.

Irrevocable Letters of Credit--a letter from a bank guaranteeing a personal check up to a stated amount.

K

Key--an assessor's term for the specific identification of a piece of property on a map.

M

Market Value--the price that property would generate in a market of willing buyers and sellers.

Mineral Rights--the right to extract minerals from land, regardless of ownership status.

N

Notice of Purchase of Real Estate at Tax Sale and of Application for Issuance of Treasurer's Deed--the document that starts the application for a treasurer's deed; also known as "Request to County Treasurer to Take Steps for Issuance of Tax Deed."

P

Premium--the amount of money paid beyond the amounts due at a treasurer's tax lien sale.

Q

Quarter--a piece of land one-quarter mile square in one of the four corners of a section of land.

Quiet Title Suit--a legal process which clears any defects or claims in a deed.

Quit Claim Deed--a deed which conveys a seller's right, title, or interest in a property, with no guarantee of ownership.

R

Range--imaginary north-south lines running along the earth's surface. In Colorado, the lines are six miles apart.

Real Property--the earth's surface, the air above the surface, the ground below the surface, and almost all attachments to the land, including buildings, structures, fixtures, fences, and improvements erected upon or affixed to the same.

S

Schedule Number--a specific number attached to each piece of property; also known as "Identification Number."

Section--a square mile of land specifically located between Range and Township numbers.

Squatters Rights--see "Adverse Possession"

T

Tax Lien--an encumbrance against a property.

Taxing Districts--geographic boundaries defining properties within a specific government city, county, state, or special district.

Title Insurance--a guarantee of ownership by a corporation.

Township--imaginary east-west lines running along the earth's surface. In Colorado, the lines are six miles apart.

Treasurer's Deed--proof of ownership.

INDEX

A

B

C

M

Market Value   49
Middleman   1
Mineral Rights   49

N

Notice of Purchase of Real Estate at Tax Sale and of
   Application for Issuance of Treasurer's Deeds   29, 49

O

Obtaining Refunds on Deposits   25
Obtaining a Receipt and Certificate of Purchase   25
One-Two Days Prior to the Sale   21

P

Premiums 23, 49
Property Addresses   18
Property Tax Assessment   31

Q

Quarter   50
Quiet Title Suit   50
Quit Claim Deed   31, 50

R

Range   17, 18, 47, 50
Real Property   50
Redeeming an Erroneously Sold Lien   28
Redemption of Liens   27
Resolution Trust Corporation   24

BIOGRAPHY

Ed Tomlinson, a Realtor for 22 years, is a top broker/associate with RE/MAX West in Arvada, Colorado. He has been researching the state's property tax lien system for over 18 years and is widely recognized as an expert in the field.

His working knowledge of the system is based on thorough study of the Colorado Revised Statutes, assessors' and treasurers' policy and procedure manuals, and training with two county treasurers.

Tomlinson has been featured extensively by broadcast and print media on a variety of subjects relating to property taxes and the status of the Colorado real estate market. He has also spoken before the Colorado Senate and House Interim Tax Committee to offer recommendations on improving Colorado's property tax system.

The author is a senior arbitrator for the Better Business Bureau, a member of the Jefferson County Association of Realtors, the Colorado Association of Realtors, and the National Association of Realtors. He has worked as a Certified Senior Appraiser with the National Association of Real Estate Appraisers.

Tomlinson also serves as a director for the Jefferson County Association of Realtors and Metrolist Inc., the supplier of Multiple Listing Service (MLS) systems to metro Denver Realtors. He is a past director of the Colorado Association of Realtors, the Jefferson County Housing Authority, and the North Jeffco Park and Recreation District. He has also served as treasurer of the Jefferson County Association of Realtors.

He is the author of the critically acclaimed, bestselling book, ***OVERTAXED! Your Guide to Honest Property Tax Reductions by Understanding and Effectively Protesting Your Assessment.***

REAL ESTATE FOR PENNIES!

Order Form

YES, I would like to order _____ copies of *Real Estate for Pennies!* at $11.95 each, plus $2 per book for shipping and sales tax.

Name _____

Address _____

City/State/Zip _____

Total Amount Enclosed _____

Please make your check payable to Diamond Publications. Send it, along with this order form, to the following address. Please allow 10 days for delivery of your order.

DIAMOND PUBLICATIONS
5440 Ward Road
Suite 110
Arvada, Colorado 80002